ICEMEN

ALSO BY VERN THIESSEN

Bluebirds
Einstein's Gift
Of Human Bondage
Pugwash
Shakespeare's Will
Vimy

ICEMEN

VERN THIESSEN

PLAYWRIGHTS CANADA PRESS

TORONTO

First edition: March 2025
Printed and bound in Canada by Imprimerie Gauvin Ltée, Gatineau

Jacket art and design by Gracia Lam

Playwrights Canada Press
202-269 Richmond St. W., Toronto, ON M5V 1X1
416.703.0013 | info@playwrightscanada.com | www.playwrightscanada.com

LIBRARY AND ARCHIVES CANADA CATALOGUING IN PUBLICATION
Title: Icemen / Vern Thiessen.
Names: Thiessen, Vern, author.
Description: First edition.
Identifiers: Canadiana (print) 20240531981 | Canadiana (ebook) 20240532902 | ISBN 9780369105424 (softcover) | ISBN 9780369105431 (PDF) | ISBN 9780369105448 (EPUB)
Subjects: LCGFT: Drama.
Classification: LCC PS8589.H4524 I34 2024 | DDC C812/.54—dc23

Playwrights Canada Press staff work across Turtle Island, on Treaty 7, Treaty 13, and Treaty 20 territories, which are the current and ancestral homes of the Anishinaabe Nations (Ojibwe / Chippewa, Odawa, Potawatomi, Algonquin, Saulteaux, Nipissing, and Mississauga / Michi Saagiig), the Blackfoot Confederacy (Kainai, Piikani, and Siksika), néhiyaw, Sioux, Stoney Nakoda, Tsuut'ina, Wendat, and members of the Haudenosaunee Confederacy (Mohawk, Oneida, Onondaga, Cayuga, Seneca, and Tuscarora), as well as Metis and Inuit peoples. It always was and always will be Indigenous land.

We acknowledge the financial support of the Canada Council for the Arts, the Ontario Arts Council (OAC), Ontario Creates, the Government of Ontario, and the Government of Canada for our publishing activities.

In memory of James Defelice.

PREFACE
DOUGLAS MOGGACH

Vern Thiessen's *ICEMEN* is a deeply local story, and yet its themes have global reach. The conflict which it describes offers a vivid evocation of a time, a place, and a set of social relations that conjure up a past era, but the play also addresses issues of work, exploitation, and inequality that continue to beset our contemporary world. Set in Barrie, Ontario, in late winter of 1936, the play depicts a town in the grip of the Great Depression, with high levels of unemployment and grinding poverty. The effects of this cyclical economic downturn are made even worse with the impending threat of technological and social change, a shift from reliance on natural resources and the labourers who extract them, to new storage techniques that will make this labour permanently redundant. The drama in this all-too-familiar situation lies in the depiction of power and resistance, the struggle, driven by dire economic constraint, to find a way out of an impossible predicament. The play brilliantly illustrates the physical and emotional effects of dangerous and debilitating labour, and the human costs of technological change.

The social issues that form the substance of the plot still resonate, but the play is also broadly based in its form, because it presents striking parallels to ancient Greek drama. Its construction recalls the three-character interactions in the tragedies of ancient Athens. Like these, the essential dramatic element is a reversal of fortune, the fall of a character from higher to lower status. The Greeks called this change *peripeteia*, derived from the verb meaning "to fall" (or, conversely, "to fly"!). In the Greek plays that have survived, these reversals, while arising directly from the preceding dramatic action, ultimately express the inexorable workings of fate or the will of the gods. Modern dramas like *ICEMEN* continue to stress reversals of condition, but now attribute these transformations not to fate but to human and social forces that drive the action and its inevitable conflicts. In the world of *ICEMEN*, two such fundamental changes occur. One of these precedes the play and provides the impetus for the plot. This first change is a slide from bad to worse in the case of the two brothers, Joe and Rennie, who, already poor, confront permanent unemployment and destitution, and so resolve on a desperate act to free themselves and to embark on a new life. The other change of fortune is that of the rich entrepreneur, F.F., who operates the local ice industry for North American markets, and who is about to abandon it to promote new refrigeration methods, dispensing with the seasonal employment on which Barrie workers depended. F.F., who is "always making up the rules," finds himself sequestered and held for ransom by Joe and Rennie and learns that it is "not pleasant being at the bottom of the rung." Which of these reversals of fortune will itself be reversed, which fall will be turned into flight and under what circumstances, provides the dramatic tension of the play.

The issue for the two brothers is power and domination, which threatens not only their livelihood but their very survival. They resist not just because F.F. enjoys wealth and commodities far beyond their reach (homes in New York and Barrie, or, as an early incident in the play illustrates, a highly valuable pocket watch) while, we are told, Rennie and Joe have none. The problem they face is that F.F. exerts ultimate power over their working lives. Rennie's debilitating injury is caused by the acceleration of the extracting machines, the length and intensity of the working day, and the lack of safety standards; and his pay is even docked for missing time due to injury. Still more importantly, though, F.F. controls access to the means of livelihood itself, to the possibility of paid employment in the ice fields. This work is about to disappear due to technical change, of which F.F. himself is the purveyor. Joe and Rennie had been driven to take seasonal work in the ice industry because of the failure of their family farm. The work, however terrible, provided income to sustain themselves and family members, including Joe's wife who is confined to a mental hospital, and his child who is in the care of his elderly father. But the days of the icemen are over: the day of freon is dawning and icemen will soon be consigned to the past. It is this threat that triggers the action of the play, where the capitalist finds himself temporarily deprived of his power to command, and subject to the control of his employees. His life hangs in the balance, and in this reversal, in his powerlessness, he is like them, dependent for survival on another person's control. In attempting to escape his predicament, F.F., the consummate businessman, resorts to bargaining, offering his captors a new sales job and the prospect of a brighter future. As they negotiate, Joe sees through the subterfuge, where competition with his former workmates would mean that none would be secure. Executing the ransom plan encounters unexpected blockages, and Joe is driven to still more desperate measures, even over Rennie's objections. The initial claim that "No one wants to hurt you. No one wants violence" gives way to darker imaginings, leading to the story's tragic denouement.

The derelict farm setting for the action of the play is not merely incidental to the plot. It is the site of an even earlier reversal of fortune that defines the social status of the characters. The inequality among them originated, by Joe's account, in a systematic theft of resources perpetrated by F.F.'s grandfather, with the complicity or indifference of the authorities. The rough subsistence equality amongst the neighbouring agricultural families was broken by a new hierarchy of wealth and its attendant privileges, arising from crime, but stabilized, normalized, and transmitted to subsequent generations through advantages of marriage, education, etc. Joe's original aim is retribution and setting matters right, taking back what had been stolen from his family; but the plan, ill-conceived as it is, risks spiralling out of control as the protagonists' actions are frustrated and the prevailing power relations prove impermeable. The reversal of fortune is reversed, at least for one of the characters, and the world beyond the farm goes on as before.

If the play makes clear the futility of the struggle in its isolated and chaotic form against dominant social relations, it elicits identification with the oppressed, with their plight and their resistance, and the hope for a better life. In this aspiration too, the play, while presenting us with memorable individual characters, reaches beyond the local in its broad, comprehensive scope. If we see ourselves in ICEMEN, we must think of another way out.

Douglas Moggach is Distinguished Professor of Political Studies and Philosophy at the University of Ottawa and is also Honorary Professor at the University of Sydney, Australia. He has taught and published extensively in the history of political thought, especially the seventeenth to nineteenth centuries. His great love is theatre, and Shakespeare in particular, awakened by a boyhood visit with his parents to the Stratford Festival, and a formative production of King John.

PLAYWRIGHT'S NOTES

A person once wrote, "People don't go to the theatre to forget; they go to remember."

I believe a theatre should program plays that are deeply connected to the people filling its seats. And so I was honoured when Iain Moggach, then artistic director of Theatre by the Bay, asked me to write a play about Barrie, a place I'd never been, and knew nearly nothing about.

Thanks to the many people I spoke with, I discovered the rich treasure trove of stories lying beneath the land Barrie sits upon and the water it lies along.

ICEMEN is born out of the sweat of three generations of Simcoe County ice harvesters who worked on Kempenfelt Bay. They saw their livelihoods taken away by greed and refrigeration, an "innovation" that over time has, ironically, contributed to the climate change that now threatens our lakes and oceans.

Like the world of my play, we are in a time of deep social and economic disparity and inequity. Like Joe and Rennie, people today are having a tough time making ends meet. Like today, there are plenty of F.F.s in the world who have too much power.

As the son of working-class immigrants, I saw first-hand the hardships of physical labour and the power of collective action. My parents taught me the necessity of unions and the dignity of hard work, lessons I have taken to heart my whole adult life.

I hope the journey of these three icemen makes you exhilarated, satisfied, and thoughtful. I hope this play reminds you of the strength of community and of the great future it holds if things are set to rights.

ICEMEN was commissioned by Theatre by the Bay Artistic Director Ian Moggach and was first produced by Theatre by the Bay on November 2, 2023, at the Five Points Theatre, Barrie, Ontario, with the following cast and creative team:

Joe: Isaiah Kolundzic
Rennie: Tom Keat
F.F.: Nathan Howe

Director: Iain Moggach
Stage Manager: Khaleel Gandhi
Assistant Stage Manager: Lesley Coo
Set Designer: Joe Pagnan
Costume Designer: Madeline Ius
Lighting Designer: Logan Raju Cracknell
Music Director and Composer: Mathew Magneson
Fight Director: Brianna Love
Dramaturge: Colleen Murphy
Production Manager: Rochelle Reynolds
Technical Director: Paul Boken
Associate Producers: Connor Jesso and Melissa MacGougan
Set Painter: Rosalind Naccarato
Props Master and Set Dresser: Brenda Thompson
Set Builder: Diane Frederick
Metcalf Intern: Sabrina Merks
Administrator: Patricia Hammond
Researcher: Mary Harris

A man may see how this world goes with no eyes. Look with thine ears. See how yon justice rails upon yon simple thief. Hark in thine ear: change places and, handy-dandy, which is the justice, which is the thief?

King Lear, Act IV, Scene VI

CHARACTERS

Joe: In his early thirties. A farmer.
Rennie: Joe's younger sibling. A big man.
F.F.: A contemporary of Joe. A wealthy man.

SETTING

Late March 1936. Simcoe County, Ontario. A utility shed on a farm.

Ice tools (e.g., picks, tongs, towing hooks, measuring sticks, augers, blades, saws, splitting bars, chisels, needle bars, grapplers) cover the wall like instruments in a medieval torture chamber. There is a stool and some battered wooden chairs, a work table, apple crates, a small pot-bellied stove, some lanterns.

NOTES

Although these characters may appear white and male-presenting, the best actors should be cast regardless of gender, race, or physical ability.

My intention is that there is no intermission between Act One and Act Two. But I would not object to it either. In total, the play should run eighty to eighty-five minutes.

ONE

Darkness.

A match.

A cigarette is lit.

In the gloom:

JOE: *(sings casually)* "Two, two cigarettes in the dark
He strikes a match till the
Spark clearly traces
One face is my sweetheart."

*The glow of the cigarette
Reveals:*

*JOE
In dirty overalls and farm boots
Smoking.*

He stokes a small stove . . .

*Its embers casting shadows
On someone nearby.*

"Two, two silhouettes in a room
Almost obscured by the gloom
We were so close yet so far apart . . . "

JOE lights a lamp.

And now we see:

F.F.
In a three-piece suit
Tied to a wooden chair
Gagged
And blindfolded.

Do you like Bing Crosby, F.F.?

Who doesn't? the question may be asked.

The grandmothers love his smooth voice
Coming in on their radios.
The ladies love his sweeping hair they see in the magazines.
The poor folk think he's a man of the people and the rich
Well
They think he's sophisticated.

Course he's no Wilf Carter.
Now *there's* a man who knows how the people
The *real* people
Live.

I'm telling you
Cowboy music is the future.

But who's to say what a person is or can be.
Am I right, F.F.?

Who knows what a person is . . .
In their *heart.*

JOE takes out a flask.

All I know is:
(takes a swig) Bing Crosby must be a rich son of a bitch.

JOE takes the blindfold off F.F.
He is coming to.
Looking about
Bewildered.

Sure, you inhaled some chloroform, but that's temporary.
Unless you mix it with the booze.
Then it can last a long time
And have effects on the brain, they say.
God knows you were piss drunk when we picked you up.
But I'm sure you've got more of a hangover than anything else.

Now F.F. is clear-headed.
He tries to wriggle out of his situation.
JOE looks about, worried.

Hey.
Calm down there.

F.F. violently tries to get out from the ropes.

Stop that now!

F.F. starts to scream through his gag.

I said HEY!

F.F. keeps screaming.

I SAID HEY!

JOE cuffs him across the face.

F.F. breathes hard.

(contrite) I warned you, didn't I?

JOE shakes out his hand.

No one wants to hurt you.
No one wants violence.
Understand?

F.F. nods.
JOE carefully examines the ropes.

Done this to a steer many a time.
Never to a man.

He tightens them some.
F.F. groans.

Sorry, F.F. Gotta be done.

He sees F.F.'s pocket watch from his vest.
Takes it.
F.F. protests.

(in awe) Look at this, then! A Hamilton pocket watch!

He bites it.

Is that solid gold?
Well, I'll be.
I'm surprised you don't have one of them new ones
You put on your wrist.

Sure, they're a pretty penny, eh?
Even *you* might not be able to afford one of those
There being an economic depression and all.
Sell this and I'd be able to buy a brand-new cow!

You remember what a cow is, don't you, F.F.?
It's where the *cream* comes from.
Or have you forgotten?

JOE *looks at the watch, winds it.*

One in the morning already.

F.F. *coughs.*

JOE *looks back.*

F.F. *coughs.*

(sincere) Soon as Rennie's back
We'll let you have a drink.
How's that?

JOE *looks at the time.*
He goes to the window, peers out.

(to self) Where you at, Rennie?
Where you at, brother?

JOE *takes a swig.*

"Big Rennie" they called him in school.
"The Jolly Giant."
Strong, Rennie is.
But a bad arm.
From the ice.
You know the story, sure.
About what happened
To Rennie
My brother?

F.F. *doesn't understand.*

No?
Well then.
I'll tell you.

Your company.
Lake Simcoe Ice and Fuel
Kempenfelt Bay.
Winter of '30.
After the big crash there in New York.
Banks call in loans.
Families lose their farms.
No work in town.
So Rennie and me do what Father did.
Harvest the ice.
No glory but it pays the bills.
(a bitter memory) Some of them that is.

Ice was good that year.
Thick.
Hard.
Shining in the sun like a plate full of diamonds.
Could see clear through it
Down to the dark waters of the bay.
White gold we'd call it

Ready to be mined.
The frozen crop.
Ready to be harvested.

Same ice you and I skated on when we was kids.
Remember those days?
Strapping on some steel blades to our boots with twine
And away we went.
Skating to school.
Lunch boxes in our mittens.
When was the last time you set foot on that ice, F.F.?
That same ice that pays for your fancy house in New York.

F.F. looks at him.

JOE takes down one of the nastier looking tools.

During the following JOE uses the tool to make points.
He gets close to F.F., painting a picture for him.

But back to my brother Rennie.
So your men
Punch holes in the ice.
It lets the water seep up to wet the snow
A crystal-clear layer scraped by a horse-drawn lathe
To make sure the ice is as perfect as can be, see?

Then they measure
Make sure it's square
Marking out grooves where the ice cakes will be
Plowing down with the Ford engine
Its big circular saw cutting two-thirds in.

Next, they separate the ice cakes from the field
Opening a channel down the middle
Creating a river

To float the cakes of ice
Toward the conveyor.

And now here's me:
At the *bottom*
Standing on a wood platform
Breaking the ice cakes into
Twenty-two by thirty inches square
Sending them up the conveyor to the ice house.

And at the *top*.
At the very top
Before the ice goes into the house
Stands Rennie
Working the planer.

You know: the planer.

Shaves off the top of the ice
Takes all the dust or bits of sludge
Makes it look like a brick of watery gold.

JOE *demonstrates its potential violence.*

It's four-bladed, see.
Four knives as sharp as the sun.
Dangerous, the planer.
Deadly if you're not careful.

And that day, F.F.
Well
Your men
They *pushed*.
Working us twenty-hour shifts.
A man gets tired, F.F.
Working that long in the bitter cold.

Mistakes get made.

So there's Rennie
Up on the conveyor
Planing the ice slabs as they come up.
But the boss man's yelling, "Faster, faster!"
And Rennie
His big body
Big arms
Big heart
Strong, our Rennie
But maybe not so fast in the head, you know?

And he's trying to keep up, see.
Trying to do his job best he can for the likes of you.
But the conveyor is going too fast for his brain.
And his arm.
It gets caught.
And the planer
Runs over it
Chewing his arm like a rabid dog.
And he's screaming
Screaming for them to stop.

And finally they do.

But his arm . . .
I'll never forget it, F.F.
Looks like a flopping fish
Alive
But gasping for breath, ya know?

Take him to the Royal Victoria in town.
Nothing they can do.
Won't take it off 'cause that would be worse.
Bind him up, send him home.

Next day?
Rennie's back!
Because that was the only thing he could do, see
To make a buck.

And your *cousin*
Jimmie.
Know what he done?
Docked Rennie a day's pay for walking out on his shift.

Then two weeks ago
Out of the blue
Boss Man Jimmie come over, say
"Last year, boys"
"Last year we'll be harvesting the ice from the bay."
And we say: "Who says?"
And Boss Man Jimmie says
"F.F. says."

And Rennie and me
And a whole lot of other people in this town
Well
We think
That's not right.
Jimmie must be wrong.
F.F. wouldn't do that to his townfolk
Not now
Not to his own
Not during an economic depression.

But it was true.
Wasn't it?

F.F. is weary, closes his eyes.

JOE will have none of that.

He grabs F.F.*'s face roughly.*

We can't have that!
Understand?

He shakes F.F.

Do you even know who I am, Frederick Forsythe?
Do ya?
It's Joe.
Joe Hewson.

We hear a truck arrive and stop.

JOE *rushes to the window,*
Leans under the sill carefully,
Peeks out.

Finally.

RENNIE *comes in.*
We see it's winter outside.
RENNIE *stomps his boots.*
His arm is in a homemade sling.

He carries a sack in and throws it down.

And a jerry can he sets down near the door.

He tosses the truck key in the air, catches it, puts it in his pocket.

RENNIE: Hey, Joe!
(casually) Oh hey, F.F. You're awake.

JOE: Where the hell were you?

RENNIE: What?

JOE: Do you know what time it is?

RENNIE: Don't own a watch. What's it matter?

JOE: Never mind. What happened?

RENNIE: Done.

JOE: Did you do like I told you?

RENNIE: Can I have a swig?

JOE: Did you?

RENNIE: Come on, Joe!

JOE hands him the flask. RENNIE draws deep.

JOE: Leave some for the rest of us!

RENNIE: Parched! Had to run, ya know!

JOE: Take some water then.

RENNIE: Ice cold.

JOE: Water don't hurt, no matter how cold. Ya put snow in your mouth all the time.

RENNIE: Okay, okay.

RENNIE takes a sip from a ladle that's in a nearby barrel.

JOE: What's with the gas can?

RENNIE: Got some extra for the truck.

JOE: Good thinking.
Now: tell!

RENNIE: Does it matter if . . .

RENNIE motions to F.F.

JOE: Don't know. He'll find out sooner or later, I suppose.

RENNIE: All right.

I did exactly like you told me, Joe. Took the note, the one you wrote. Tied it to a rock. Stood in the dark, sixty feet from the window. Just like I was pitching to home plate. Waiting. Waiting. Then just as I seen F.F.'s wife pass by the window, I threw a pure curveball, Joe. Oh it was a beauty. Over and around through the yard, and BASH, through the glass. Just like in the old days. A pure strike. And no one could tell where it came from.

F.F. is concerned.

F.F. starts to curse under the gag.

JOE: It's tragic, F.F.
What happened to Rennie.
He was a helluva ball player, weren't ya.

RENNIE: *(blushes)* Aw, Joe.

JOE: You was.
Scouted by the Stratford Nationals, he was.
You can still throw, Rennie.
Even with your bad hand.

RENNIE: You mean my good one.

JOE: The only one you *can* throw with.

RENNIE: That's what I mean.

JOE: See? So don't you worry.
Rennie's got good aim.
You didn't hurt F.F.'s wife, did you?

RENNIE: No way!

JOE: Mamie—that's her name, isn't it? And the kids, you didn't hit little Frederick Forsythe the fourth, did ya?

F.F. is breathing heavily—furious.

RENNIE: Ya know I wouldn't do that, Joe!
(to F.F.) I'd never do that, F.F.

F.F. is mad as hell.
Stamping his feet.
Thrashing about.

Whoa, whoa there.
(panicked) Joe? What'a we do?

JOE goes over to the barrel
Picks up a ladle of water
And throws it in F.F.'s face.

JOE: *You quiet down!*
You shut your mouth.
And your feet there.
Or else.
(to RENNIE) Anyone see you?

RENNIE: Quiet as a kitten.

JOE: Good.

F.F. is coughing now, almost choking.

All right, all right.
Rennie.
Get him a cup of water.

RENNIE does.

Now
I'm gonna undo this.
But you raise your voice a note too loud
I'll stuff it all the way to the back of your throat.
Understand?

F.F. nods, coughing.
JOE undoes the gag.
F.F. coughs violently.

F.F.: *(raw)* Water. Please.

RENNIE looks and JOE nods.
RENNIE gives him sips of water.
It takes a while.

Finally, F.F. gets his breath back.
He's relieved.

JOE: There now.

He's about to put the gag back on.

F.F.: No, please, Joe. Not that again. Please. I'll do what you say. Please.

JOE looks to RENNIE.

RENNIE: I believe him, Joe.

JOE: All right then. But any yelling and it goes back on, ya hear?

F.F.: Thank you. What about my arms and legs?

JOE: Don't think so.

F.F.: Can you just loosen them for a moment? The ropes are cutting off my circulation. Please.

JOE nods to RENNIE, who begins loosening them with his one good arm.

JOE: Just a little, Rennie.

F.F.: Can I ask you one question, Joe?

JOE: Sure.

F.F.: *WHAT THE HELL ARE YOU DOIN'?!*

JOE: Now I warned you.

F.F.: Seriously! What's this all about? I have no clue, no clue how I got here, *what* you two are up to, or *why* you're doing it. I think I'm entitled to some answers, for Chrissakes.

RENNIE: No need to swear.

F.F.: No need to— I've been kidnapped, bound, gagged, taken to a place I know not where, water thrown in my face—*I got every reason to swear my goddamn Christly head off!*

JOE: Last chance or the gag goes back on.

F.F.: *(trying to stay calm)* For the love of God, boys.
What. Are. You. Doing?

JOE: Nothing you need to know!

F.F. looks to RENNIE.

F.F.: Rennie, then *you* tell me. What are you and your brother up to?

RENNIE looks to JOE, who shakes his head no.

RENNIE: Can I tell him, Joe? Just a little? I mean, maybe F.F.'ll understand. Maybe he'll help us. He's gonna find out anyway.

JOE hesitates. Takes a swig.

JOE: All right. But not too many details!

RENNIE revels in this:

RENNIE: Okay. So. We read in the *Northern Advance* you were coming back from New York for the big Icemen's Conference at the Queens Hotel on Dunlop there. And so we waited outside, see. We parked our truck across the street and down a ways, by the cenotaph. And we watched. And we seen all you icemen, on the balcony there, smoking cigars, sipping whisky, out of a glass yet, puffing away into the dark, on a warm winter night, no moon, you and the other icemen, laughing, laughing . . .

JOE: That's a pretty picture you paint, Rennie.

RENNIE: Thanks, Joe.

F.F.: But how did I . . . ?

RENNIE: Joe and I wait. We wait for all you icemen to finish your eating and drinking and talking. And most of those out-of-towners from Buffalo and Toronto and Cleveland, they're staying at the hotel. But not you, F.F. You got your big house up on Peel Street. Everybody knows that. And we see you stumbling out of the Queens Hotel and take a right down Dunlop toward the Five Points piss drunk, singing to yourself . . .

JOE: *(as a drunk* F.F.*)* "Two, two cigarettes in the dark
He strikes a match till the spark . . . "

RENNIE: I'm not a Bing Crosby person myself. If I gotta listen to that kind of music, I'll take Guy Lombardo. He's Canadian, you know. Or Wilf Carter.

JOE: That's what I said!

RENNIE: "Pete Knight's Last Ride"! That's my favourite.

JOE: *(sings)* "It seems my whole life's full of sorrow and sighs"

RENNIE: *(sings)* "Always something make me feel blue"

JOE: *(sings)* "For I just lost a pal like a brother to me"

RENNIE & JOE: *(sings)* "I still can't believe that it's true."

They try a yodel. They laugh.

F.F., *steamed, can barely contain himself.*

F.F.: What. Happened.

RENNIE: Right. So you're walking home and Joe and I pull up and Joe says:

JOE: "Fred! Frederick Forsythe! It's me! You remember me!"

RENNIE: And you pretend like you do, and we're like:

JOE: "Let us give you a ride home. Looks like you could use one!" And you climb in the front seat.

RENNIE: And I chloroform you. I was sitting in the back, see.

F.F.: Yeah. I got that.

JOE: Lots of chloroform on the farm. For when we need to put an animal down. We can't afford bullets for the gun anymore so we gotta use an axe, and we don't want them to suffer see, so . . .

RENNIE: Worked like a charm, didn't it, Joe.

JOE: Like a charm.

F.F.: *(frustrated)* But for what REASON?

RENNIE looks at JOE.

RENNIE: Let me tell him, Joe.

JOE: Tell him what?

RENNIE: The reckoning.

JOE: *(considers)* Yeah. Go ahead. This might be a good lesson for F.F.

RENNIE: I done the reckoning.

JOE: He's done the reckoning, Rennie has, because he may be slow at some things, like getting his hand out of the ice planer, but he's real fast at figuring out how much something's worth. Like that ice house down on Mary Street. Your ice house. How much it worth, Rennie?

RENNIE: A lot.

JOE: There ya go. A lot. How much, Rennie? How much did you reckon?

RENNIE takes out a soiled piece of paper and a stubby pencil.

RENNIE: Let me explain it on paper: a team of twenty-five men can take a thousand tons of ice from an acre of Kempenfelt Bay. Every day.

JOE: A thousand tons. Every single day.

F.F.: I don't need a lecture on how much my business makes in a—

JOE: Shut your gob! Go on, Rennie.

RENNIE: A thousand tons of ice a day. And last year, for example, which was a good year, we worked one hundred and ten days on the ice.

JOE: A hundred and ten days.

RENNIE: So that's one hundred and ten thousand tons of ice in that house.

JOE: Over a hundred thousand tons, and to think, there are some houses that take upward of two hundred, even three hundred thousand. Keep going.

RENNIE: Last year, the price of ice was a dollar for a thousand pounds. So that means . . . that ice house of yours is worth . . .

He double-checks his math.

Two million dollars.

JOE: Two. Two MILLION dollars! And it's free! Mother nature giving up her bounty every cold day in Simcoe County from January to March. Now, Rennie, how much we make harvesting that ice?

RENNIE: A dollar twenty-five an hour.

JOE: But we got paid by the day this year, remember. No extra pay for staying on the floe overnight.

RENNIE: Eleven dollars a day.

JOE: Seventy-seven dollars a week to be precise. And even if we *could* harvest year-round, we'd still only be earning four thousand a year. So, you see what we're getting at here, F.F.?

F.F.: No, I don't actually. First of all, that's the commercial rate of ice.

JOE is not pleased. He moves toward F.F.

No, please, Joe, come on now, really, let me say *something*. That price, that was for the high-end customers: the hotels, the railways, the politicians. We never charged ordinary folks that. Hell, we even gave ice for free to some!

JOE: Did you now?

F.F.: Sure, to the people at the hospitals and the asylum in Penetang and Beeton and to the veterans of the war. We gave away lots of ice for free.

JOE: How generous of you.

F.F.: It's not cheap to get that ice to market. Not only you fellas to pay, but the ice houses to build and getting them to market on the train before they melt, all the equipment, the insurance . . . Well, *you know*, it's like running a farm! You don't think about the chicken, you think about how much you can charge for the eggs at the market.

JOE: Or the beef.

F.F.: Sure, or the beef. I guess.

JOE lights a smoke.

JOE: I wouldn't know, F.F.
'Cause it's been a long time
Since we ever taken anything to market.
And even if I did
Someone there'd probably have something for cheaper.
But that's not the case with the ice, is it?

F.F.: What'd'ya mean?

JOE: You fix the price of that ice.
Don't you.
You and your icemen.
That's why you're here.
To decide what ice costs.
Even though you get it for free from Kempenfelt Bay.

F.F.: We didn't get it for free—that's what I'm trying to tell you! And yes, we fix the price, not so it costs more, but so it's *fair*. To everyone. The folks in New York and Buffalo, they can afford to pay more, the people here in Barrie, they can't. We're trying to make it *fair*.

JOE: Ha! Fair!
You people.

JOE spits on the floor.

Always doing the talking.
Always making up the rules.
Business this and business that.
And that's all it is:
Busy-ness.
It's not work you do.
It's keeping busy being greedy.
That's your job, after all
To make the most money
Am I right?

F.F.: Of course you're right.
Because I got *my* own bosses I gotta answer to.

RENNIE: Your bosses?

F.F.: That's right!

JOE: And who might they be?

F.F.: The shareholders of the company. *Those* are my bosses. The investors, the big players, the tycoons, the Du Ponts and the Carnegies and the Rockefellers. They want their money back on their investment and then some.

JOE: So what I'm hearing is that you, F.F., are just a cog in the money-making machine, is that right?

F.F.: Exactly.

JOE: Well, if you're over here in this machine

JOE indicates high.

Rennie and me and the men working the ice, we're down here.

JOE butts his smoke under his foot.

Right?

F.F.: That's right. We all have a place on . . . the ladder.

RENNIE: Well, say someone wanted to climb up that ladder. How's a guy like me or Joe supposed to get to the next rung?

F.F.: Well, it's not that easy. You gotta have money to invest.

RENNIE: And how I get that?

F.F.: You raise it.

RENNIE: From where?

F.F.: From all kinds of places: people you know, investors, borrow it, your savings.

RENNIE: *(honestly)* Savings? What's that?

F.F.: The first thing you need to do is get an education.

JOE: Ah ha! There we go. An education.

F.F.: Of course. Everyone in this county, if he wants it, can have a good education.

RENNIE: *(honestly)* Did I get a good education, Joe?

JOE: Sure you did, Rennie.
In life.
And look at you now and how you reckon.
You're very good at maths.

F.F.: I still don't know why I'm here!

JOE: Patience, F.F.
Not pleasant being on the bottom rung, is it?
Not nice being the one who doesn't make the decisions.
Not fun being the one who gets told what to do
And when to do it.
Is it?

F.F. turns to RENNIE.

F.F.: Why'd you throw a rock through my window, Rennie?

RENNIE: Why? 'Cause it had a note attached to it.

F.F.: What note?

RENNIE: The note Joe wrote.

JOE: Rennie.

F.F.: What that note say, Rennie?

RENNIE: It said—

JOE: Nothing. It said nothing.

F.F.: What you so scared for, Joe? I'm tied up here. I ain't going nowhere. What's it matter now? Like Rennie says, I'm gonna find out anyway. Like Rennie says, maybe I can *help* you.

JOE: Like your grandfather helped mine?

F.F.: *(perplexed)* What?

JOE looks at F.F. Studies him.

RENNIE: Maybe he can help, Joe?

He nods to RENNIE.

JOE: But when I say shut up, you shut up, ya hear?

RENNIE nods.

RENNIE: So I threw the rock through the window.

F.F.: At my wife.

RENNIE: No, sir, I made sure not to hurt nobody.

F.F.: Were you trying to hurt her?

RENNIE: No, I said!

F.F.: That broken glass could have hurt her. That rock could have ricocheted off a wall or something.

RENNIE: I was careful!

F.F.: She's with child, ya know.

JOE: What?

F.F.: We just found out.

JOE: You're lying.

F.F.: She's in the family way, I tell you. And you threw a rock at her.

RENNIE: I DID NO SUCH THING.

F.F.: Did you see my boy?

RENNIE: No. Upstairs asleep, I figured.

F.F.: I can't believe you'd—

RENNIE: She wasn't hurt.

F.F.: How do you know that.

RENNIE: 'Cause I saw. I saw her pick up the rock and look out the window. And she was fine. She turned back and I heard her yell something and that's when I took off. I swear, F.F., I did not hurt her. I'd never do nothing to hurt a lady or a kid, would I, Joe.

JOE: No you would not.

F.F.: And what was attached to the rock? A note, you say?

RENNIE: Yes.

F.F.: And what did that note say?

> *RENNIE looks to JOE.*
> *JOE considers.*
> *F.F. looks to JOE.*

Well?

JOE: Let's see what F.F. has to say to the note. I'm curious.

F.F.: What did it say?

RENNIE: The note said: "We have F.F. Come to Queen's Park ball diamond at 6 a.m."

JOE & RENNIE: Before the sun rises.

JOE: "Come alone. Bring fifty thousand dollars in cash in a suitcase. Drop it beneath the bleachers behind home plate. Leave. We will know when you are gone."

RENNIE: That's it.

F.F. looks at them both.

He starts to laugh.

JOE doesn't like this.

F.F.: *Fifty thousand dollars? Fifty thousand . . . Are you two mad?*

JOE: It's a drop in the bucket of that two million, isn't it?

F.F.: *(laughs)* Oh for the love of . . . fifty . . . And if they don't?

JOE: That lovely ice house on Mary Street?

JOE lights a match.

Poof.

F.F.: And you don't think I'll *tell* people who did it?

JOE: You won't be alive to.

F.F. looks at him.

F.F. looks at RENNIE.

He tries stay in control.

F.F.: . . . Now wait a minute.

RENNIE: Can I have a smoke, Joe?

JOE: Sure. Better yet. Let's see what F.F. has.

JOE digs in F.F.'s coat.

Finds a cigar.

Look at this! Old Havana! Ever had a cigar, Rennie?

RENNIE: Don't think I ever have. Not a good one, anyways.

JOE tosses RENNIE the cigar and matches.

RENNIE lights it. Pockets the matches.

He puts his feet up and enjoys being the boss.

F.F.: You can't be serious.

JOE: It's a good deal.

RENNIE: Remember last year? When those fellas kidnapped that John Labatt?

JOE: Chained and blindfolded him out at that cottage in Muskoka.

RENNIE: Turned chicken.

JOE: Yes they did. Got spooked. Let him go.

RENNIE: Without the money!

JOE: Stupid buggers.

RENNIE: They got fifteen years EACH at Kingston.

JOE: So we won't be making that mistake, will we, Rennie?

RENNIE: *(laughs)* I sure hope not, Joe.

JOE: No we will not.

F.F.: *(to RENNIE)* I thought you said you didn't hurt people.

RENNIE: *(honestly)* Women and children, F.F. I mean, I kill animals all the time on the farm.

F.F.: You're, you're going to kill me? Over some *ice*?

JOE: Oh, but it's not just *ice*.
Is it?
It's money.
Big money.
Or you wouldn't be treating those men out there
The likes of Rennie and me
You wouldn't be treating us like we were a cigarette
Stomped out under your boot.
And now with the company shutting down
We can't even strike for higher pay
Like the men did back in the '70s.
So what choice do we have

To "work our way up the ladder."
You tell me.

F.F.: Killing me is not the answer.

JOE: That's only if we're forced to.

RENNIE: *(gently)* And we'd chloroform you before. Like I do with the animals. You wouldn't feel nothing.

F.F.: You two really *are* insane, you know that? It's you they should be sending to Penetang!

JOE: It's a nice touch, the baseball field, don't ya think? Rennie had a future on that field, and it was taken away, and now here we are, levelling it.

F.F. calms himself.

F.F.: Okay. Okay. Right now. Can I . . . Can I have a swig, please? Can you give me that?

RENNIE looks at JOE and nods.

RENNIE goes over and puts the bottle to F.F.'s lips.

He swigs. Motions for another. Gets one.

Okay. Gentlemen. *Gentlemen*, I say. Will you hear me out? Can I just . . . Just let me ask you some questions. Okay? Let's start there.

RENNIE: What kind of questions?

F.F.: Easy ones, I figure.

RENNIE: Easy questions are easy to answer, right?

F.F.: Exactly. Joe?

JOE: Go ahead. Don't mean we have to answer them.

F.F.: All right. Question one: What if my wife doesn't see the note till the morning? What then?

RENNIE: Oh, I seen all the lights go on. I watched her through the window looking at the note.

F.F.: All right, question two: How do you think she is going to get fifty thousand dollars in cash overnight.

JOE: Oh, come on, F.F.
By now, Police Chief Skinner knows.
He's woken up every iceman at the Queens Hotel!
He's woken up the bank manager at the
Toronto Dominion on Yonge Street.
You think we're stupid?
You think between all of them
They can't collect fifty grand overnight?

F.F.: Okay, fine. Question three: Do you not think they are going to be staking out that ball diamond from every corner? They'll have police surrounding the place from Ross to Parkside to Toronto Streets. You think they're going to let you walk away with fifty thousand dollars at six in the morning?

JOE: I think the instructions were to "come alone."
So when Rennie goes down there before dawn
He's gonna check things out, aren't you, Rennie?

F.F.: That's right, Joe.

JOE: And if he sees even one person out on that street
In the cold of winter
At 6 a.m. before the sun is up
He's gonna know he's a policeman.
Because even the drunks aren't wandering around that early.
And if they are well
Rennie'll be leaving.
And your ice house will be burned to the ground
With you in it.

F.F.: Last question. You get the money. What the hell are you going to do with it? I'm going to tell them it's you. You won't get away fast enough for them not to find you. You couldn't go a hundred miles without getting caught, that old jalopy of yours. And what are you going to do with that money? You wouldn't know what to do with fifty dollars let alone fifty thousand. And what if they *don't* give you the money? You gonna burn down the ice house with me in it, and then what? Go back to your lives on that lousy little farm in Innisfil? You aren't any further ahead. Either way, they'll catch you. They'll have you in the Barrie jail in no time. And you *know* how many people been hanged in the Barrie jail. This county never had any problems hanging people.

RENNIE stands up.

RENNIE: Joe, is he telling the truth? They gonna hang us?

JOE: Shush now.
(to F.F.) Well let me answer your questions as best I can.

If we get the money
We'll be leaving you here
Drugged up on the chloroform.
We'll make sure you can lick some water out of a bowl
And bite on a raw potato
And after a few days

If they haven't found you
Or you haven't escaped
We'll make sure they find you.
You'll be hungry and thirsty and smelly.
But that's no different than Rennie and I are today.
Isn't that right, Rennie?

RENNIE: I'm always hungry, Joe.

JOE: I know you are, brother.
It's because you're a big man with a big heart and a big appetite.
Did you bring those potatoes?

RENNIE: I did.

JOE: Well feel free to munch on one.

> RENNIE *goes to the bag he brought in and takes out a raw potato.*
>
> *He brushes off the dirt, takes a pocket knife, trims off a piece, takes a bite. He continues doing this while he speaks.*

RENNIE: I remember when we'd have enough potatoes and corn and beans, the whole family could eat well, and we'd still have enough to sell in Barrie at the market?

JOE: I do too.

RENNIE: I remember when the cattle could feed well, and we'd have enough beef the family could eat well, and we'd have enough to sell some to the butchers in Allendale?

JOE: I remember.

RENNIE: I remember when we were happy to just be farmers and didn't need to worry about no economic depression and folks just lived nice and simple.

JOE: Those were good times, Rennie.

RENNIE: I miss those days. I miss old Barrie. I miss old Innisfil and old Allendale. What changed, I wonder?

F.F.: What *changed*? The *world* changed! Listen to you two! Wishing for a world that's *gone*! You gotta think ahead, you gotta think forward, you gotta look to the *future*. That's why we're shutting down the ice business. Because the next thing is freon.

JOE: What's that? Freon.

F.F.: It's artificial ice, like. It's like ammonia but safe. General Motors and DuPont, they're making it so we don't *need* to take the ice off Kempenfelt Bay. We can refrigerate things without using ice. Within a decade all those ice businesses will be gone. *That's* what we were talking about at the Queens Hotel. How we shut down our ice businesses and move to freon.

RENNIE: You shut up with this talk.

F.F.: It's the truth, Rennie.

RENNIE: Only God can make ice, you hear me?

F.F.: No stopping it.

RENNIE paces, angry.

RENNIE: I said shut your mouth!

F.F.: *DO YOU KNOW WHO I AM?*

JOE: *(amused)* Do tell!

F.F.: I am a CAPTAIN OF INDUSTRY.

JOE: *(laughs)* A what?

F.F.: I am one of the wealthiest men in Simcoe County. I have used my God-given talents, and abilities, and wealth, and *hard work* to create something for myself *and* for the reputation of this shabby, mean, dirty little town. A town stuck in the barrens of northern Canada. A town with nothing of value to it but the thick and brutal ice that freezes on the godforsaken plane of Kempenfelt Bay.

JOE: *(wryly)* You have to admit, it's lovely in the summer.

F.F.: I'm not here because I need to be. I have a perfectly good life in New York. I can board an ocean liner to Europe or Cuba whenever I want. But I don't. I don't. I keep my family here, and a house here, and my children here, because, by God, this terrible place has given me my wealth, and no matter how much I hate it, I owe it to this place to do good here—to try and raise it up, to help build schools and churches, to give to the poor, to employ the likes of you two, when I could bring in workers for half the price from the States, to honour my roots, even when I don't care to spend time with them, to give back something to this place that may raise it to a level of respect, of notoriety, of LOVE.

RENNIE is becoming more agitated.

I've done everything in my power to bring some semblance of humanity and dignity and culture to this place that was only good enough for you poor, disgusting, decrepit, immoral Irish immigrants, who couldn't do anything here but grow potatoes and raise poor cows, their scrawny carcasses passing for beef. And for this you kidnap me? For this—?

RENNIE has moved slowly and deliberately on F.F.

He grabs F.F.'s neck with his good hand.

And nearly lifts him out of the chair.

It's the first time we've seen his gentle nature vanish and replaced with a terrifying temper.

RENNIE: *(coldly) I told you to shut your mouth!*

F.F.: *(scared)* . . . Joe?

RENNIE: I want things to stay the way they are or go back to what they were. I don't want no more changes, you understand me?

F.F.: Joe . . . do something, will ya?

RENNIE: *(cold and calm)* We're not disgusting. Or any of those other things you said. Our house was a *clean* house, and our farm was a *beautiful* farm, a *happy* home until someone started stealing our cattle, and spreading bad rumours about our family, and dragging our good name through the mud, and the bank won't give us any more loans.

And *now* you want to take away what little we have in the winter, the ice on the bay, and you're not even planning to replace that work with anything, are ya? What are we gonna do without that work? WHAT? We're losing everything because of people like you. Taking away our hope.

F.F.: *(choking)* Sure, Rennie, sure.

RENNIE: So you take back what you said about us, or I'll choke you dead just like I do the chickens on the farm.

RENNIE's big hand is starting to squeeze.

F.F.: I'm hearing you, Rennie. I'm . . .

JOE: Easy, Rennie.

F.F.: Joe! I'm . . .

F.F. can't breathe.

JOE: Let him be now, brother.
We've got him where we want him.
Easy there.

JOE gently takes RENNIE's arm down from F.F.'s neck.

RENNIE slowly let's go.

His anger changes to regret.

JOE rubs his back to calm him.

RENNIE: Sorry.

JOE: That's all right.

RENNIE: I don't like to hurt no one.

JOE: We know that, Rennie. You're the Gentle Giant.

RENNIE: I am. I don't like getting angry, it's not like me. But sometimes . . .

JOE: We know.

RENNIE: I don't like being treated bad.

JOE: And no one should treat you bad. Right, F.F.?

F.F.: Sure, Rennie.

RENNIE: I'm sorry. I truly am. And you know I'd never hurt Mamie, or her unborn child, or F.F. the fourth. I wouldn't.

JOE: Course you wouldn't.

RENNIE: All right then.

Things have calmed. JOE *turns to* F.F.

JOE: So, as you can see. We're serious about all this.

And to answer all your questions:

As to where we go:
Well of course, I won't be telling you that.
But as you know there are plenty of options around here.
North into the woods.
West over to Georgian Bay and down to the US.
South to Toronto where it's easy to disappear.

And as for using fifty thousand dollars.
Well, Rennie is good at reckoning.
Who knows, maybe it'll take us back to Ireland
Where my great-great-great-great-grandfather was born
Before he came to settle these parts.
You'd *love* that, wouldn't you, F.F.?

F.F.: *(quietly)* You don't stand a chance.

JOE looks at F.F.'s pocket watch.

JOE: But look at the hour.
Time to sleep.
All of us.
And then before you know it
It'll be time for Rennie to go into town.
And see what fate awaits us.
Rennie?

JOE motions.
RENNIE gets the chloroform.
Gets the cloth.

F.F.: No, please, Joe. I'll sleep. I'm tired. I don't need it. I swear I won't try anything.

JOE: Sorry, F.F. We can't take no chances.

F.F.: Did you not hear what I said? I'm doing this all for YOU.

JOE: And I don't trust a man who talks about his high and mighty morals while he's picking my pocket.
Be gentle now, Rennie.

RENNIE: Just take a deep breath.

RENNIE does the number on F.F.
F.F. struggles but RENNIE is gentle and takes only a few seconds.

I don't like getting angry, Joe.

JOE: I know. Forget it now. Did you bring the blankets?

RENNIE: I did.

JOE: Throw one over him so he doesn't get too cold. And loosen his wrists and arms just a little.

RENNIE: Okay, Joe.

RENNIE takes out the blankets from the sack.

JOE: Toss me one.

RENNIE does.

Then he attends to F.F., making him as comfortable as possible.

Throw a few potatoes into the embers. They'll cook nice. We'll need to eat something before morning.

RENNIE: Okay, Joe.

JOE: And lay out your blanket. Get some shut-eye.

RENNIE: Okay, Joe.

JOE: But don't sleep too deep. You just want to nap so you can rise and get into town before six.

RENNIE: I got enough gas now to get me there and back and some extra in case we need it.

JOE: Good.

He does what JOE has asked. It takes some time.

When RENNIE has done all his things
He lays a blanket on the ground by the dying embers.

JOE goes to him.

He takes RENNIE's bad arm.
Massages it gently.
He tucks his brother in
As he has done since forever.

RENNIE: Joe?

JOE: Yeah?

RENNIE: Was that true, what F.F. said?

JOE: What do you mean?

RENNIE: Are we alive because of the likes of him?

JOE: If it is, we gotta change that.

JOE puts out the lamp.

The embers light their faces.

RENNIE: If we get the money, where *will* we go?

JOE runs down the plan as facts:

JOE: First: we're gonna walk.

RENNIE: Where?

JOE: Across the bay.

RENNIE: Over the ice?

JOE: Toward the rising sun
Our long shadows
Like giant trees.

RENNIE: Okay.

JOE: Then:
We'll walk to Snake Island
Then Georgina
And there we'll rest.
When we're ready
We'll walk to Thorah Beach
Then to Beaverton
Where we buy supplies.

Then:
We head
Deeper into the land
Where the Wendat still live.
Until we're in the Kawarthas.
And further still
Until we're in the land of Algonquin Park.

We'll make camp there for a while
Where they'll never find us.

And when the time comes
We'll change our names
And head down to Kingston.
Finally: we'll cross over the river
To the States
And make our way to Syracuse.
And there we'll start our own business.
And we'll never look back.

RENNIE: But I like looking back.

JOE: Maybe F.F. is right:
Maybe we gotta look ahead.

RENNIE: If you say so, Joe.

JOE curls onto the table with the blanket.

JOE: But first, we'll walk to the east.
And before you know it . . .
We'll be free.

The embers burn down to darkness.

TWO

The pre-dawn light slowly slips into the shed window.

RENNIE *is gone.*

As is the jerry can.

JOE *is asleep.*

F.F. *is awake, looking about for a means to escape.*

He tries various things:

Wriggling his hands out of the ropes.

No luck.

Twisting his feet backward and forward against the chair.

Not working.

Hopping with the chair closer to a sharp instrument on the wall.

One hop. Checks on JOE.

Second hop. Checks on JOE.

Still asleep.

One more and he'll be close.

Third hop.

A little too loud.

JOE *stirs.*

F.F. *is panting from the work.*

JOE *awakes.*

JOE: Ah. You're awake. How'd you sleep?

F.F.: How do you think.

JOE: Where's that Rennie?

JOE *checks the pocket watch.*

I gotta piss.

He slides into his boots and heads out.

He sings from off:

"We were old pals on the prairie,
Many times we have rode side by side
Never dreaming a bronco would throw him
And that Pete Knight would take his last ride."

JOE *tries yodelling.*

Alone, F.F. *looks about.*

He spots the knife that RENNIE *used to cut the potato.*

Can he make it? He tries one more hop.

He's close, but then . . .

JOE *comes back.*

I see you've made some movement.
Getting your morning exercise?

F.F.: It's starting that I can't feel my feet, Joe.

JOE: We'll fix that soon.
Beautiful morning for a ransom.
The sun coming up over Cook's Bay—

F.F.: Cook's Bay?

JOE: Ah! Look at me, giving away our location a little.

F.F.: We're in Innisfil?

JOE: The less you know the better.

F.F.: Joe, I got to go myself, you know?

JOE: Do you now.

F.F.: It's been a long time, and I was drinking last night.

JOE *considers.*

You want me to piss my pants, Joe? Come on.

JOE: I'll untie one of your hands so you can pull it out.
The other stays tied behind your back.

F.F.: And how'm I getting out there?

JOE: I'll untie you from the chair.
But your feet stay tied.
I figure you can't hop your way to New York.

F.F.: Thank you.

JOE does this carefully and does the least he needs to.

JOE: Let's see.

F.F. hops to the door, which JOE opens.

F.F. hops out.

JOE watches from the door.

There ya go.
Good man.
Give the snow some of the booze ya drank last night.
It'll be thankful for the colour.

JOE looks at the watch. Considers it.

Tell me, F.F.
Your boy . . .
Does he have a red Ohio Tin lunch box.

F.F.: *(calling)* What's that?

JOE: A bright red tin lunch box with sports figures on it. Hockey and baseball players, kids on a toboggan.

F.F. has hopped in.

F.F.: How'd you know that?

JOE: 'Cause it was yours. Wasn't it? When you was a kid.

F.F.: Why are you asking about that now?

JOE motions and F.F. hops his way back to the chair.

During the following JOE goes to the stove and takes out the potatoes. Then he stokes the embers.

F.F. looks to the knife.

JOE: Because.
Your grandfather and mine farmed cattle next to each other.
Here in Simcoe County.
Your granddad was the shrewd Scot
And mine the hard-living Irishman.

F.F.: What is this, a history lesson?

JOE: Not a bad thing to know your history, F.F.

They were good farmers and cattlemen.
Both bred fine cows
High-end Angus.
For the beef.
Selling it to the butchers
In Allendale and Barrie
Even Orillia.

F.F.: What does this have to do with my kid's lunch box?

JOE: I'm getting there! Boy you Scots are impatient.
So there they are:
Your grandfather and mine
Neighbours.
Shared a drink or two, I'm sure.
Debating the better whisky, no doubt.
Helping each other out
As neighbours should.
But then . . .

JOE lights a smoke.

Something happens.

F.F.: Do tell.

JOE: Suddenly
Your grandfather gets rich
And mine gets poor.

F.F.: Ha. Just like that.

JOE: Just like that.
Like it was overnight.
Soon my da
Can't send me to school in Barrie anymore.
Have to stay back and work the farm.
Don't get past grade seven. But!

But for that short while
You and I's classmates.
Back when you was just Fred

And not Frederick Forsythe the third.
Back when we ate together lunch behind
Prince of Wales Public School
Me with my piece of bread and butter
And nothing else
Wrapped up in some old newspaper
And you
You with your red Ohio Tin lunch box
With all those sports figures on it
Got from the Eaton's catalogue or somewhere
Your parents had to *pay money* for it.
And inside your box:
Cheese
And a glass of *buttermilk*
And a piece of *chocolate.*
So you see
Even then
You and I wasn't equal.

F.F.: All this because of a lunch box? Is that what we're saying?

JOE: You're rich, F.F. But you're not really very smart, are you?

I'm talking about *cows*, F.F.
I'm talking about how one day
Your granddad
Goes over to *our* pasture
At *night*
To take a cow.
Slaughter it, send it to market
Make money
As if it was his.

F.F.: Wait. You're accusing my family of *cattle rustling*?

JOE: Oh, I'm not accusing.
I'm telling what's *fact*.
The first time my granddad does the count
He thinks one has gone stray in winter
Died of exposure, fell in a slough
That kind of thing.
But then every few months
Another Angus gone.
Then every few weeks
Until Granddad knows something's wrong.

F.F. shakes his head in disbelief.

So he goes down to the butcher's
And sees the brand of our cattle
The upside down "J"
For Joseph
On a leftover piece of rump
About to be burned
With the rest of the offal out back.
And he asks the butcher
"Why you selling stolen beef?"
To which the butcher replies
"We don't care where it's from. We need the meat."

So my grandfather goes to your grandfather
To present what he's seen
And your grandfather
Says to mine:
"If you're so sure
Go to the chief constable. Make your case."

And so my grandfather
Goes to see Chief Constable Rogers
And when he asks for evidence
My grandfather shows him the leftover rump

With the J brand on it from the butcher
And that we did not deliver it there
And the chief constable
With his fat face and big belly
Hems and haws and then says:
"Well, you know, Hewson,
The Forsythe beef
Is far better than yours anyway.
You're the one should be stealing from *him.*"

And my granddad punches the constable
Straight in the mouth
As it's clear the good-for-nothing chief
Is being paid off by your grandfather.
In beef.

F.F.: If I had two free hands to clap, I'd do it, Joe. Hell, I'd get on my feet. I'd whistle for an encore. What a fiction! This was told to you by your da to make up for the fact that he gave you nothing. He drank down everything he made on that farm and left you with nothing but a worn-out house and a barn sinking to its knees.

JOE: How do you think your da came up with a dowry
That he could marry the rich daughter of
The good Reverend McCann, huh?
He of St. Andrew's Presbyterian on Owen and Worsley Streets.
He the president of the Royal Victoria hospital.
He friend to ministers of another kind
Those in Her Majesty's Government of Ontario.
He of the wealth that not only comes from being nearer to God
But also to the rich and powerful of Simcoe County.

They talk on top of each other:

F.F.: He worked for it, unlike yours.

JOE: Your grandfather didn't have that kind of money.

F.F.: He earned it, I tell you.

JOE: He could have worked himself smart to the bone
His whole goddamn life
He'd *never* have enough cash to cozy up to the rich.

F.F.: *Don't you talk about my father like that!*

JOE: *Nothing* would stop him from making sure
F.F. the second
Moved up in the world
Or it'd be a life of hard hands and long winters
Holed up on a farm
With nothing but the land
And the wind
And chickens
And cows
As his future.

F.F.: Fine, fine. Even if this ridiculous story *were* true, what's it to do with me? Am I guilty of the sins of my father, or my grandfather?

JOE: You haven't come to your wealth honestly.
Don't you see that?
Your grandfather was a thief
And a liar
And he stole so his son
Your father
Could move up in the world
Move up that ladder we were talkin' about.
And your father went up it
Oh yes he did.
He married up

And his business went up
And he made a fortune being a
Lumber baron
In these parts
And made enough so that you
His son
Could leave Barrie and become
A millionaire in New York
On the backs of the people of this county.
You're a crook, F.F., plain and simple.

F.F.: *(furious)* If I had two hands free.

JOE: What would you do, F.F.?
Hit me?
Call the cops?
Hell, jail don't look so bad when you got nothing to eat.
No, no, *sue* me, huh?
That's what you people like to do.
Sic lawyers on each other.
Problem is, I got no money to settle.
No, you got nothing to hurt me.

F.F.: *What the hell do you want from me?*

JOE: *I want back what your family stole!*
I want my boy to have a red Ohio Tin lunch box with sports players on it! I want what's mine, that's what I want!

F.F.: Wait, you got a boy?

JOE, caught, looks away.

What's his name?

JOE: None of your business.

F.F.: Tell me.

JOE: *None of your business.*

JOE goes to the window and peers out.

He checks the watch.

F.F.: What time is it?

JOE says nothing.

Is he late?

JOE checks the coals. He lays the watch on the stove.

What do you think happened?

JOE: Nothing.

F.F.: Maybe he's taken the money and run.

JOE: What?

F.F.: I'm just sayin'.

JOE: Don't speak bad of my brother.

F.F.: I'm just saying what if he doesn't come back, then what?

JOE: *(threatening)* You're talking shite is what you're talking. And I'll none of it, ya hear?

JOE takes a swig of the whisky.

F.F.: Let me have a little, would ya, Joe. It's been a long night.

JOE gives it to him.

F.F. drinks. It's strong.

F.F. sighs. Tries another tack:

He's lucky, that Rennie.

JOE: Why's that.

F.F.: He's got freedom. He can do whatever he likes. Not like us. We're fathers. No doubt Mamie's worried. And she having a baby coming. And I'm gonna miss Freddie play piano tonight.

JOE: Piano?

F.F.: Yeah. He's been taking lessons from that Mrs. Hayes in town. Every year they have a "recital," what they call it. Where they have to play some songs or other. I don't care for it much, but it's taught him patience and confidence.

JOE: *Piano* taught him all that?

F.F.: And Mamie gets to show off her little man. Anyway, not sure what they'll do tonight if I don't get home. Tell you one thing, you're gonna have one mad woman at you, Joe Hewson, for making her cancel a party for her son.

JOE: Well at least you got someone worried or mad at you. Don't take that for granted.

F.F.: What's your wife's name again?

JOE is silent.

And your son, what's he called then?

JOE is silent.

He's nine now, Freddie. That's what Mamie calls him. He's a good lad, sharp as a tack, and loves playing baseball. Just like your brother.

JOE: *(to himself)* Huh.

F.F.: Not very good at it, mind, but he loves the *game.* Knows all the players on all the teams. Loves Lou Gehrig and Hank Greenberg. He spends his summers with me in, well, in New York, and we go see the Yankees play sometimes. He knows all their batting averages and runs and such.

He's good at the maths and science, and he likes the stars, Joe. I got him this telescope, and winter nights he sits up late searching the sky above Kempenfelt Bay. Knows all those constellations and can tell you all about the planets and such. Dreams of being an "astronomer." Can you imagine us, Joe, as kids, dreaming of being an astronomer?

JOE: Can't say I did. I didn't have no dreams when I was a kid.

F.F.: Nothing? Not even—

JOE: Feeding my family—that was my dream. Making sure there was food on our plates.

JOE touches the potatoes.
They've cooled.

I guess you're hungry, am I right?

F.F.: I could eat.

JOE: Here.

He gives F.F. *a potato. They munch.*

Is he kind to his mother? Your boy?

F.F.: *(surprised by this)* Sure, and courteous too.

JOE: That's good.
That's really good.
Sounds like he's growing up smart and happy.

F.F.: He is.

JOE: My boy.

JOE considers.

He's turning seven next month.
He's stubborn, our Jack.
You can't tell him nothing.
Wonder where he got that from.

They laugh a little.

They pass the bottle back and forth once or twice.

He goes off on his own into the woods
Snares rabbits
Brings home odd and old-looking rocks
Sometimes turtles and snakes.
He loves the earth, that boy.
Would spend an entire night alone out there if I'd let him.
Staring at the stars.
Loves the farm
Rides a pony like he was born on it
And names the cows
What's left of them . . .

He hesitates.

F.F.: And your wife. What's her name again?

JOE: Nora.
Met when we was twelve.
Best friends since we were kids.
Went to school together.
Till we both had to stay back to mind the farm.
She was from the Foley family in Stroud.
Bred Angus, just like us.
Fine-boned, Nora.
Skin like fresh milk and hair red as a rooster.
Got married at St. Mary's RC as soon as we were legal.
Da gave us some of his land
And the Foley's some of their cows to get a start.

F.F.: Where's Nora now, Joe? I mean, does she know what you're up to here?

JOE: I . . .

It got so bad, see, I . . .

I had to send them away.

Couldn't feed them no more.

And Nora
She
Well
She already lost three before Jack was born . . .

F.F.: Good Christ.

JOE: She wasn't well in her head.
So we sent her to rest.
In Beeton.

F.F.: *(aghast)* At the manor there? The House of Refuge?

JOE: What choice did I have?
It doesn't cost nothing.
And my father and grandfather are there.
Taking care of Jack.

F.F.: And if you get the money?

JOE: I'll send for him.

They drink.

F.F.: Joe. I got a question:
Why didn't you just ask me for the money?

JOE: What's that now?

F.F.: Why didn't you just ask me for the fifty thousand dollars.

JOE: Ha!

F.F.: Well?

JOE: Ha!

F.F.: What's so funny?

JOE: You really think that little of me, don't'cha?
You think I've got that little pride?

F.F.: And you're proud of this?

JOE: I'd rather *take* my share than be a beggar.

F.F.: So now *you're* the thief.

JOE: This isn't stealing. It's making things right. There's a difference.

> F.F. *thinks.*

F.F.: Come work for me, Joe.

> JOE *looks at him, agog.*

I'm serious. You're a smart man. You know the business. The ice business that is. Pretty soon every housewife in this county is going to want her own icebox. But it won't be the icemen delivering it anymore. It'll be their own box, with freon in it, keeping things cool with electricity and that's it.

JOE: What is this nonsense now.

F.F.: You'll make a ton of money the *first year* selling freon to the county, Joe. Think about it: a new life, a new future, for you and for Jack. And maybe you'll get Nora out of Beeton to a calm and comfortable place.

JOE: Ha! Can you imagine? Me? Walking around with airs? Selling things?

F.F.: You said it yourself: you know the people. And I don't. You're right—I'm too far removed from the plain folk around here. But you! You can talk to them in their own language. You have their trust. They'll believe what you say.

JOE: I gotta take care of Rennie.

F.F.: That's easy! He's big and strong. He could be a bodyguard even with that bad arm. I could, I could set him up in New York working for a baseball club. Hell, I'd sponsor his *own* team right in Barrie if he wanted. All you need to do is tell him what's what. Whatever you say, he'll do.

JOE: Where'd I live then? If not at the farm.

F.F.: Anywhere you want. A little house in Barrie? We'll buy it for you. I'll arrange for the big money in New York and you run the local part of the business in Simcoe County. Once they figure how to mass-produce these iceboxes with freon—and they say it's maybe six months off—all the housewives are going to want one. Like the car, or the radio, one in every house by the end of the decade.

JOE: So I'd be a salesman.

F.F.: That's right.

JOE: And how much's that pay exactly.

F.F.: Well let's do some reckoning, shall we? How many homes in Simcoe County?

JOE: No idea.

F.F.: All right, I'm going to say there are at least five thousand homes. Would you agree?

JOE: Okay.

F.F.: And let's say these new ice boxes cost a hundred and fifty dollars each.

JOE: A hundred and fifty! You gotta be kidding me.

F.F.: Why? Cheaper than their yearly ice bill now.

JOE: True.

F.F.: Five thousand homes times a hundred and fifty is seven hundred and fifty thousand dollars. And let's say you get a commission of ten percent.

JOE: Commission?

F.F.: On every unit you sell. You'd make seventy-five thousand dollars. And that's a conservative estimate.

JOE: Huh.

F.F.: You see? We're *not* all that different, you and me. Both born here. Both want better things for our wives. *And* sons. Both want to make a go of what we're good at. We both know what it feels like to want to get ahead. To do better for ourselves and our community. What do ya say?

> F.F. *stands, holds out his free hand to seal the deal.*

> JOE *stares at it. Then moves his hand toward* F.F.

> F.F. *grabs it, shakes it.*

Good. That's great. Look at us. Our granddads would be proud, don't ya think?

> *Something twigs in* JOE.

JOE: Our grandfathers, huh?

F.F.: That's right.

He doesn't let go of F.F.*'s hand.*

JOE: So. Wait. Did I hear you right? I only get paid if I sell one?

F.F.: That's the way business works these days, Joe. Bigger risks, bigger rewards. And of course, you'd be competing against all the other salesmen.

JOE *squeezes* F.F.*'s hand hard.*

JOE: What other salesmen?

F.F.: Well, you wouldn't be the only one for the county.

JOE: Why not?

F.F.: Well, that's called a monopoly, Joe. And businesspeople don't like that.

JOE: Well, you got the monopoly on ice prices, don't'cha? Why not set a solid wage?

F.F.: You gotta have competition, Joe.

JOE: Oh, so now I'm in "competition" with who exactly? Who else is selling these iceboxes?

F.F.: I don't know.

JOE: Oh, I think I do.

F.F.: Who?

JOE: The other men who worked the ice.

He finally lets go and pushes F.F. *back into the chair.*

F.F.: That's possible, I guess.

JOE: Because what are they gonna do when the other ice companies shut down? They're all going to be in my shoes, aren't they?

F.F.: They're not our problem.

JOE: You gonna give them jobs too?

F.F.: Aw, come on, Joe.

JOE: No, I'm serious.

F.F.: Don't you see what I'm offering you here?

JOE: Oh I see it all right.
Half of those men are too old
Or too uneducated to do anything else but the ice.
So they'll what
Go on relief, I guess.
And then another quarter will just plum up and leave
'Cause there's no future for *them* here.
And the rest will start in maybe on this new freon business.
So now I'm trying to sell your newfangled icebox
While a buncha other fellas
People I know
Are doing the exact same thing.
And we'll be trying to sell them to people who have no money.
They can barely grow enough food, let alone have an icebox.

And the more of these things they make
The more the price's gonna come down
Am I right?

F.F.: Joe.

JOE: So now instead of making that seventy-five thousand dollars
It looks like I'm making maybe half that
Or a quarter
Or ten percent
And then I'm back where I started.
And meanwhile you
And your friends in New York
Protect yourselves
Because in the end
You own it.
And now you're pitting us people against each other
And wrapping it all up in a nice bow called "the future."
It's always the poor people who get to experience the future last.
Aren't I right, F.F.?

F.F.: Joe.
Listen to me.
I'm trying my best here.
I'm trying to make it so I can walk out of here alive, and you and Rennie can walk out of here with a future that's not being in a cold cell in Kingston Penitentiary.

JOE: No.
No.
You see, F.F.
Watching them
Take Nora
Kicking and screaming into that place in Beeton
Screaming out my name
Dropping off Jack at my grandparents'
His lip quivering
And me saying:
"Don't you worry now.

"It's all right. We'll get there. We'll get there."
And looking into his eyes
Not knowing where we were going to get to
And how we were going to it.

That's when I knew.

I had to do something.
Or we'd be stuck
Like horses in high snow
Freezing to death.
On the inside and out.
That's when I realized that you and me
We're never gonna be the same
We're never gonna be equals
Until we both have the same things.

F.F.: And what are those?

JOE: Money and power.
Before today
People like you had both those things
Over people like Rennie and me
In spades.
But not today.
Today I got both.
And I don't plan on giving up either.
And I'm sure as hell not interested in sharing.
So to hell with your "deal."
I'm the only one making deals now.

They hear the sound of the truck.

JOE *runs to the window, ducks down just in case.*

Meanwhile F.F. *grabs the knife from the table and quickly hacks his way through the ropes.*

He pockets the knife and situates the ropes as if he is still tied.

It's Rennie, all right.
And no one following him.
Ha!
He's got a crate with him!
Ha!

JOE *opens the door.*

F.F. *looks around.*

What to do?

Run, use one of the ice picks?

Too late:

RENNIE *lugs in a small crate.*

Places it on the table.

Leaves.

What took you so long?

RENNIE: I just gotta get the . . .

He comes back quickly with the jerry can.

JOE: What happened?

RENNIE: It took some time was all. The driving back. Taking all those detours we talked about. And time to get more gas. Just in case.

JOE: *(relieved)* Right. Good thinking. You're sure you weren't followed?

RENNIE: Sure as I could be, Joe.
(humoured) Were you worried, Joe?

JOE: Me? Never.

> RENNIE *places the truck key in his pocket.*

> JOE *looks out one more time.*

> *A bare glance at* F.F.

RENNIE: Hello, F.F.

F.F.: Hello, Rennie.

RENNIE: It all went smooth, Joe. Got to Queen's Park. Checked all the corners. No one. It was dark. I snuck through that grove of trees behind the diamond and under the bleachers. And that's where it was. Took it, put it in the truck, and bolted. Took all the corners and alleys you told me, then I took the 20th Sideroad back here like you said.

F.F.: 20th Sideroad?

> *They ignore him.*

JOE: Good, brother, you done good.

RENNIE: We need a bar to open this. They nailed it shut good.

RENNIE goes to the wall.

F.F. is doing a good job of pretending to still be tied up.

JOE: An ice pick'll do it.

RENNIE grabs one.

JOE lifts the box—it feels the right weight.

So, F.F., this is what fifty thousand dollars feels like in your hands, huh?
But I guess you'd know that.

RENNIE starts to crack it open.

Wait. Wait. Let's make a toast first.

JOE climbs on an apple crate.

To our grandfathers
And our fathers
And to us
And to all our sons and daughters of the future:
May this be the day the tides turn in our favour
And become a blessing for our people.

He drinks.

RENNIE: Now?

JOE: Now.

RENNIE starts to crack open the box.

Well, F.F., are you excited as I am, to have your freedom?

F.F.: I sure am, Joe.

RENNIE: What the . . .

RENNIE has cracked open the top and is looking inside.

JOE: Well?

RENNIE: *Ah no. No!*

RENNIE throws down the wooden box lid.

JOE: What?

JOE goes over.
Looks inside.

RENNIE: *Those bastards. Those sons of BITCHES.*

F.F.: What is it?

JOE lifts out a part of what's in the box:

JOE: *(quietly)* It's ice.
It's a block of ice.
To make it feel
You know . . .
The *weight* . . .

He shows F.F. the block.

Oh they are clever
Your friends
Aren't they?
So clever.

RENNIE: What's this?

> RENNIE *has found a note tacked to the underside of the lid he threw down.*

JOE: A note.

RENNIE: What's it say?

> JOE *unfolds it.*

JOE: "We don't negotiate with thugs. F.F. understands."

> JOE *looks at the note, then at* F.F.

Well, well.

F.F. understands, does he?

> *He turns on* F.F.

What exactly does F.F. understand?

> F.F. *jumps to his feet, knife in hand, ready.*

F.F.: F.F. understands a lot of things.

RENNIE: How'd he—?

> RENNIE *checks for his knife. Realizes:*

Awwww!

JOE: Rennie! The calipers!

> RENNIE *grabs them from the wall.*

JOE has the ice pick.

They are now all armed.

It's not going to be easy for F.F. to make an escape.

What do you understand, F.F.? I'm curious to know.

F.F. is cornered.

F.F.: F.F. understands they're not giving you the money on principle.
F.F. understands their principles are more important than my life.
And F.F. understands his life's in his own hands.
That's what he understands.
Now
You can let me go
And I won't say a word . . .

JOE: *(laughs)* Is that a fact.

F.F.: Or you can kill me
And burn down that ice house
For nothing.

JOE: Revenge ain't nothing.
You remember what they done to the Black Donnellys
Down in Biddulph Township.
No one ever convicted anyone in that fire.
Isn't that right, Rennie?

RENNIE: I wouldn't know, Joe.

JOE: Well you do now.

They move in.

F.F.: Now, fellas, listen to me.

They disarm him quickly.
JOE *turns the knife on* F.F.

Think about Freddie, Joe! Think about my wife and the one to come. Think about Jack!

JOE: Rennie.

RENNIE *places the calipers around* F.F.*'s head like a vice.*

F.F.: For God's sake, boys!

JOE: Do ya know, F.F.
These ice calipers.

They can grab a three-hundred-pound cake of ice
And never make a dent in it.
That's how hard the ice is from Kempenfelt Bay.
That's why it's so valuable.
But a human head
Is much
Much softer
Wouldn't you say, Rennie?

RENNIE: *(honestly)* I'd say that is correct, Joe.

JOE: Rennie, while you were gone, F.F. offered us jobs.

RENNIE: Huh.

JOE: Yessir. He offered us a new life. A life where we'd make a lot of money.

RENNIE: Doin' what?

JOE: Selling stuff for him.
Being his *employees*.
He'd even give you your own baseball team if you wanted.
Fancy that.

RENNIE: You ain't gonna take a job from him are ya, Joe? That'd be—that'd be a betrayal, it'd be wrong, after what he done to our family, to us, to me, to my arm.

JOE: Good points, Rennie.
You always were smart.
In your heart.

RENNIE: Why doesn't he just give us that outright? Why we gotta work for him?

JOE: A good question.

He motions to RENNIE *to let go.*

Why don't you give us all that?
Give us all that you offered with no conditions
Or shady employment.
Give us the baseball team
AND the seventy-five thousand dollars
And we'll call it even.

F.F.: You know I can't do that, Joe.

JOE: *(threatening)* And why the hell not?

F.F.: Because. I can't just . . . People are going to ask questions. They're going to ask "who held you" and whatnot. And I'm, what, I'm going to shut my trap and then, poof, there's a new ball team with Rennie's name on it?

JOE: Then we'll just take the seventy-five thousand dollars.

F.F.: Joe, I don't have that kind of cash—not even in the bank! It's all held on credit. I buy stock, I sell stock to pay the bills, I get credit on my assets, but I don't deal in *cash*, no captain of industry deals in cash anymore. It's not couth.

> JOE *is furious. He grabs* F.F. *by the hair in one hand and the chair in the other and drags him to the table.*

JOE: Rennie, give me your pencil and that paper they sent.

> RENNIE *does so.*

Now this is what you're going to do, F.F.
You're going to write a note.
Here *(the pencil)* and here *(the paper)*
Write what I tell you.

> F.F. *has the paper and pencil. His hand is shaking as he writes.*

"To whom it may concern."

F.F.: *(writing)* To whom . . . it may . . . concern

JOE: "Be prepared to deliver seventy-five thousand dollars in cash. By tomorrow morning at 6 a.m."

F.F.: *(writing)* Be prepared to deliver . . .

JOE: In cash!

F.F.: *(writing)* . . . in cash by . . . 6 a.m. . . .

JOE: "Or we kill F.F.
And his son."

F.F. stops.

F.F.: *(quietly)* What?

JOE: Write it.

F.F.: No. No.

JOE bangs his hand on the table.

JOE: *Write it!*

RENNIE: Joe, I don't think . . .

JOE: WHAT? What don't you think?

RENNIE: Joe . . .

JOE: Never mind. I'll finish writing it.

JOE grabs the note and pencil.

Knock him out. We're going into town.

RENNIE: Both of us?

JOE: We're going to F.F.'s house to get that boy.

F.F.: For Christ's sake, Joe, please.

JOE: We'll toss that note in the house, nab him, put him under, blindfold him, and bring him back here.

F.F.: They're going to see you, Joe.

JOE: We'll wear our scarves—like balaclavas.

F.F.: You've gone mad!

JOE: If we have to kill you and your boy
Well
You've still got another on the way, don't'cha?
Your name will live on.
It's called "lineage" I believe.
And they can still use your goddamn special red lunch box.

RENNIE: Joe . . .

JOE: What?

RENNIE: Not the kid, Joe.

F.F.: That's right. That's right, Rennie.

RENNIE: That ain't right. Not the kid.

F.F.: Ya see, ya see? Even Rennie knows it's not right.

RENNIE: We can't be killing kids, Joe.

JOE levels the ice pick hard against the table.

JOE: *SHUT UP! BOTH OF YOU!*

He levels the ice pick against a chair.

(to F.F.) You're going to find out how we feel
Every day of our lives.

The Fear.
The Shame.
The Rage.

F.F. makes his final desperate move.

He kicks JOE's feet from under him, who falls.

F.F. picks up the ice pick and swings it at RENNIE.

Catching him on his good arm.

RENNIE falls, wincing.

JOE is on one knee and slashes F.F. on the leg with his knife.

F.F. turns with the ice pick.

JOE attacks and F.F. reacts mechanically and without malice.

He stabs JOE. And immediately drops the pick.

Oh God.

JOE falls.

RENNIE: Joe!

RENNIE runs to JOE.

F.F.: I didn't mean . . . It was an accident!

RENNIE: Joe!

JOE is bleeding badly from the stomach.

F.F.: Jesus.

He looks around.
Goes to the door.
Looks out.
Turns back.

Where's the key to the truck, Rennie?

RENNIE *is holding* JOE.

I know where we are now. We're at your farm. Or what's left of it.

RENNIE *doesn't answer.*

The key, where the hell is it?!

RENNIE *doesn't answer.*

Listen. I'll bring back help.

RENNIE *looks at him.*

I, I promise.

RENNIE *looks at him.*

What have you got to lose?

RENNIE *looks at him.*

Reaches in his pocket.

Throws the key.

F.F. *takes it.*

He sees his watch on the stove—takes it.

He looks at them.

(with disgust) . . . You people.

F.F. *spits on the floor.*

He hobbles out.

The sunrise is now burning its way into the shed window.

We hear the truck start up and drive off.

RENNIE: Joe? Joe, can you hear me?

JOE *is breathing, but it doesn't look good.*

JOE: It's all right, Rennie.
It's all right.
We'll get there.
See?
We'll get there.

RENNIE: Joe?

JOE*'s eyes roll back.*

Joe?

RENNIE *shakes* JOE.

Joe?

JOE *does not respond.*

RENNIE weeps.

What am I gonna do now, Joe?

RENNIE calms.

RENNIE thinks.

He wriggles out from beneath JOE.

He is the one who tucks his brother in now.

As he does:

(sings) "Oh some day there will be a great round up on high
When the ranch boss starts combing the plains,
May our names all be square on the tally
May we meet on that heavenly range."

He spots the jerry can.
Goes to it.
He splashes gasoline around the shed.

We're gonna walk, Joe.
Like you said.
We're gonna walk across the bay.
We're gonna walk toward the rising sun.

RENNIE digs in his pocket.
He pulls out the cigar.
He lights it. Takes a puff.

And before you know it . . .
We'll be free.

And throws it down.
A growing blaze.

As the ice in the apple crate
Screams with rage.

End of play.

ACKNOWLEDGEMENTS

Thanks to Iain Moggach and the entire production team for their outstanding work on the premiere. Thanks to all the people in Barrie who spoke to me about their love for the community and its future. Thanks to Susie Moloney, Michael Moloney, and Louise Casemore for helping me with early drafts. Thanks to Colleen Murphy for her inspiration, theatrical courage, and assistance with dramaturgy on the play. Thanks to all the artists who participated in readings and workshops of the play. A special thanks to Mary Harris, who was instrumental in helping me research these men and the conditions and times they lived in.

Vern Thiessen is one of Canada's most produced playwrights. His plays have been seen across Canada, the UK, United States, Europe, Australia, New Zealand, and Asia and been translated in seven languages. His works include *Of Human Bondage*, *Vimy*, *Einstein's Gift* (GG winner), *Lenin's Embalmers* (GG finalist), *Apple*, and *Shakespeare's Will*. He has been produced off-Broadway five times. Vern is the recipient of numerous awards, including the Dora and Sterling awards for Outstanding New Play, the Carol Bolt Award, the Gwen Pharis Ringwood Award, the City of Edmonton Arts Achievement Award, the University of Alberta Alumni Award of Excellence, the Canadian Jewish Playwriting Competition, and the Governor General's Literary Award for Drama, Canada's highest honour for a playwright. He was also a finalist for the Siminovich Prize in Playwriting. Vern received his B.A. from the University of Winnipeg and an M.F.A. from the University of Alberta. He has served as president of both the Playwrights Guild of Canada and the Writers Guild of Alberta. For six years he served as Artistic Director of Workshop West Playwrights Theatre, one of Canada's leading new play companies. He is married to acclaimed screenwriter and novelist Susie Moloney.